CHARLES B. & PATRICIA A.

TUBBS

CHILDREN'S

LIBRARY

First Facts™

From Farm to Table

From Milk to Ice Cream

by Kristin Thoennes Keller

Consultant:
H. Douglas Goff, Professor of Food Science
University of Guelph
Guelph, Ontario, Canada

Capstone press

Mankato, Minnesota

First Facts is published by Capstone Press
151 Good Counsel Drive, P.O. Box 669, Mankato, Minnesota 56002
www.capstonepress.com

Library of Congress Cataloging-in-Publication Data
Thoennes Keller, Kristin.
  From milk to ice cream / by Kristin Thoennes Keller.
  p. cm.—(First facts. From farm to table)
  Includes bibliographical references and index.
  ISBN 0-7368-2635-1 (hardcover)
  1. Ice cream, ices, etc.—Juvenile literature. [1. Ice cream, ices, etc.] I. Title. II. Series.
TX795.T49 2005
637'.4—dc22   2003023372

Summary: An introduction to the basic concepts of food production, distribution, and consumption
    by tracing the production of ice cream from milk to the finished product.

Editorial Credits
Roberta Schmidt, editor; Jennifer Bergstrom, designer; Kelly Garvin, photo researcher; Eric Kudalis,
    product planning editor

Photo Credits
Capstone Press/Gary Sundermeyer, front cover, 5, 19
Comstock Inc., back cover, 1
Corbis/Richard T. Nowitz, 10–11; Roger Ball, 16–17
Corel, 20 (left)
Grant Heilman Photography/Grant Heilman, 8
Lynn M. Stone, 6–7, 9
PhotoDisc Inc., 20 (right)
Richard T. Nowitz, 14–15
Washington State University Creamery, 12, 13

1 2 3 4 5 6 09 08 07 06 05 04

Table of Contents

A Cool Treat

Many people enjoy eating ice cream. They eat it in cones or dishes. People also enjoy ice-cream **products**, like ice-cream sandwiches.

Ice cream has to be made before people can eat it. Making ice cream takes many steps.

Fun Fact!
Vanilla is the most popular flavor of ice cream. Chocolate is the second most popular flavor.

Ice Cream Starts with Milk

Ice cream is made from milk. Milk comes from cows. A cow's body makes milk after it gives birth to a calf. Milk is the calf's food. A cow can make more milk than the calf needs. People can use the extra milk. It is sometimes made into milk products like ice cream.

Fun Fact!
Cows are female cattle. Male cattle are called bulls.

Getting Milk

Most farmers use machines to milk their cows. The milk flows through pipes. The pipes carry the milk to cooling tanks.

The milk stays cool until milk trucks pick it up. The trucks take the milk to **dairies**. There, some milk is used to make ice cream and other milk products.

Making Ice Cream

Ice cream is made of many **ingredients**. Milk and **cream** are the main ingredients. Most ice-cream makers add sugar, color, and flavoring. All of the ingredients are put in a large tank. The ingredients are blended together to make the **mix**.

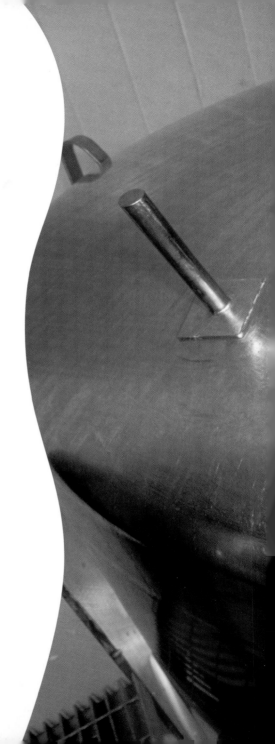

The Mix

After the mix is blended, it moves through pipes to another machine. This machine heats the mix to kill any **bacteria**.

Then the hot mix travels to another machine. This machine breaks the fat in the milk into smaller bits. The mix becomes smooth and creamy.

Freezing and Adding

The mix travels to a freezer. A machine whips air into the mix as it freezes. The air keeps the ice cream from getting too hard.

Some kinds of ice cream have fruit, nuts, or cookies in them. These ingredients are stirred into the mix as it freezes.

Fun Fact!
Premium ice cream has less air and more fat than other ice cream.

To the Store

Machines squirt the ice cream into cups, **molds**, or other containers. The containers are put in a colder freezer. The ice cream becomes very hard.

Freezer trucks take the ice cream to stores. The stores keep the ice cream in large freezers.

Fun Fact!
July is National Ice Cream Month in the United States.

Where to Find Ice Cream

People can buy ice cream almost anywhere food is sold. Grocery stores sell many kinds of ice-cream products. Smaller stores, like gas stations and drugstores, also sell ice cream. Some shops sell only ice cream.

Fun Fact!
The first ice-cream cone was made in New York in 1896 by Italian American Italo Marchiony.

Amazing but True!

George Washington loved ice cream. In the 1700s, ice cream was a rare treat. One summer, Washington spent $200 on ice cream. That's the same as nearly $100,000 today.

Hands On: Ice Cream in a Bag

You can make your own ice cream at home. Follow this recipe to make ice cream in a bag.

What You Need

ice cubes
1 gallon-sized (3.8 L-sized) sealable plastic bag
6 tablespoons (90 mL) rock salt
½ cup (120 mL) milk or half & half
¼ teaspoon (1.2 mL) vanilla
1 tablespoon (15 mL) sugar
1 pint-sized (0.5 L-sized) sealable plastic bag

What You Do

1. Put the ice cubes into the large bag until the bag is half full. Add the rock salt. Seal the bag.
2. Put the milk, vanilla, and sugar into the small bag. Seal the bag.
3. Open the large bag. Place the small bag inside the large bag. Seal the large bag again.
4. Shake the bags for about 5 minutes or until the mix becomes stiff.
5. Take the small bag out of the large bag. Wipe off the outside of the small bag. Open the small bag and enjoy your ice cream.

Glossary

bacteria (bak-TIHR-ee-uh)—small living cells; some bacteria can cause diseases.

cream (KREEM)—a thick, fatty liquid found in whole milk

dairy (DAIR-ee)—a place where milk is bottled and milk products are made

ingredient (in-GREE-dee-uhnt)—an item used to make something else

mix (MIKS)—the blend of ingredients for ice cream

mold (MOLD)—a shaped container

product (PROD-uhkt)—something that is made; ice-cream products are made from ice cream; milk products are made from milk.

Read More

Cooper, Elisha. *Ice Cream.* New York: Greenwillow Books, 2002.
Landau, Elaine. *Ice Cream: The Cold Creamy Treat.* Tasty Treats.
Vero Beach, Fla.: Rourke, 2001.
Older, Jules. *Ice Cream.* Watertown, Mass.: Charlesbridge, 2002.

Internet Sites

FactHound offers a safe, fun way to find Internet sites related to
this book. All of the sites on FactHound have been researched by
our staff.

Here's how:
1. Visit *www.facthound.com*
2. Type in this special code **0736826351**
   for age-appropriate sites. Or enter a
   search word related to this book for
   a more general search.
3. Click on the **Fetch It** button.

FactHound will fetch the best sites for you!

Index